‖‖ ‖ ‖ ‖ ‖‖‖‖‖‖‖ ‖‖‖‖‖‖ ‖‖‖‖ ‖ ‖‖
AF200068

Impressum
Verlag: BABADADA GmbH, Nedderfeld 112 , 22529 Hamburg
Geschäftsführer / Verlagsleitung: Harald Hof
Druck: Books on Demand GmbH, In de Tarpen 42, 22848 Norderstedt

Imprint
Publisher: BABADADA GmbH, Nedderfeld 112 , 22529 Hamburg, Germany
Managing Director / Publishing direction: Harald Hof
Print: Books on Demand GmbH, In de Tarpen 42, 22848 Norderstedt

school

sekolah

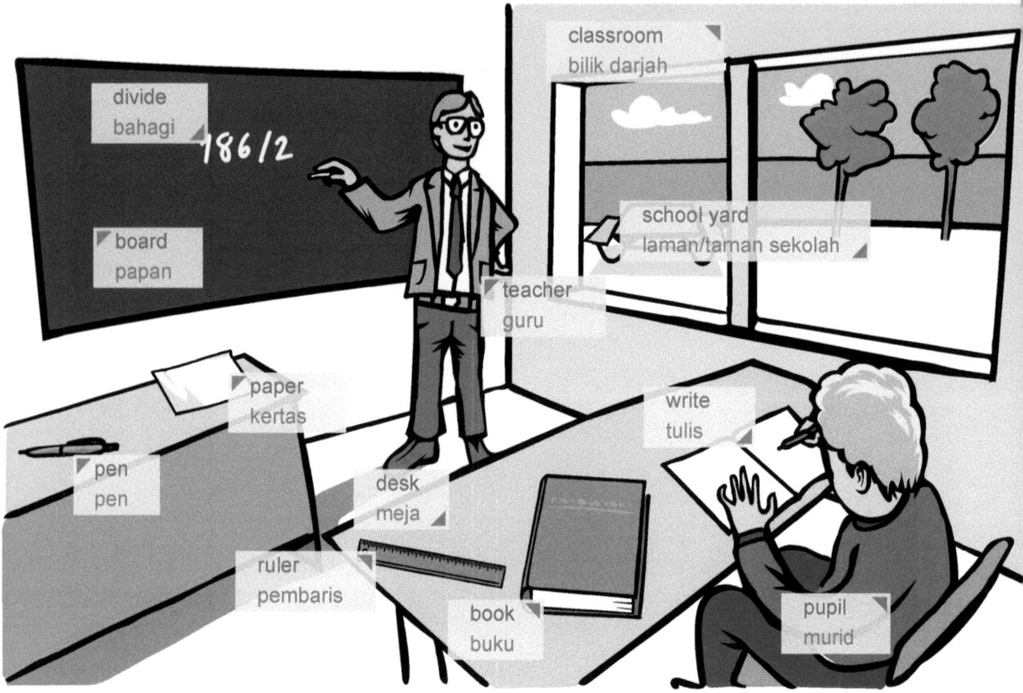

classroom
bilik darjah
divide
bahagi
186/2
board
papan
school yard
laman/taman sekolah
teacher
guru
paper
kertas
write
tulis
pen
pen
desk
meja
ruler
pembaris
book
buku
pupil
murid

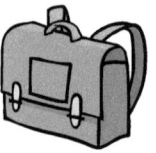

satchel

beg galas

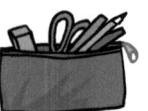

pencil case

kotak pensel

pencil

pensel

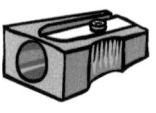

pencil sharpener

pengasah pensel

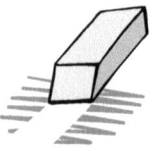

rubber

pemadam

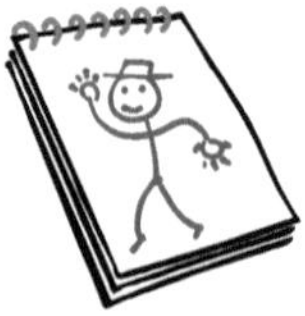

drawing pad

kertas lukisan

drawing

melukis

paintbrush

berus lukis

paint box

kotak warna

scissors

gunting

glue

gam

exercise book

buku latihan

homework

kerja rumah

number

nombor

add

tambah

subtract

tolak

multiply

darab

calculate

kira

letter

huruf

alphabet

abjad

word

kata

text

teks

read

baca

chalk

kapur

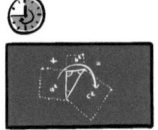

lesson

pelajaran

register

daftar

exam

peperiksaan

certificate

sijil

school uniform

uniform sekolah

education

pendidikan

encyclopedia

ensiklopedia

university

universiti

microscope

mikroskop

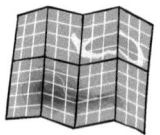

map

peta

waste-paper basket

bakul sampah

hotel
hotel

Grand

hostel
asrama

ROOMS

bureau de change
pejabat tukaran mata wang

ECHANGE

car
kereta

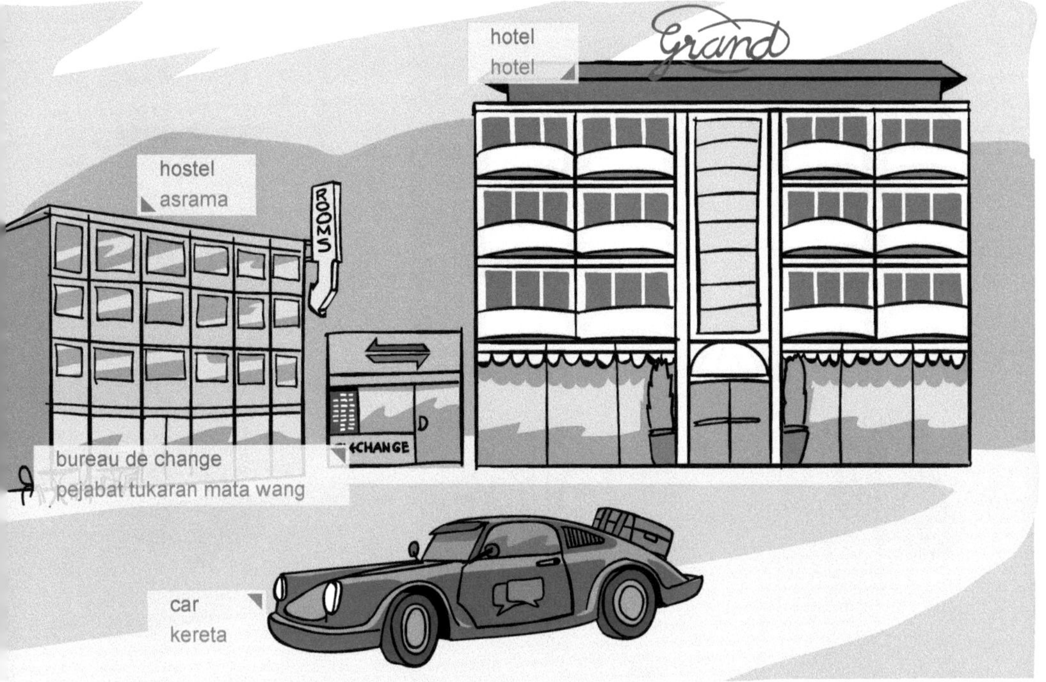

language

bahasa

yes / no

ya / tidak

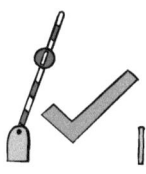

Okay

okey

hello

helo

translator

penterjemah

Thank you

Terima kasih

how much is...?

berapa banyak...?

I do not understand

saya tidak faham

problem

masalah

Good evening!

Selamat petang!

Good morning!

Selamat Pagi!

Good night!

Selamat Malam!

bye bye

selamat tinggal

direction

arah

luggage

bagasi

bag

beg

backpack

beg galas

guest

tetamu

room

bilik tidur

sleeping bag

beg tidur

tent

khemah

travel - berjalan

tourist information
maklumat pelancong

beach
pantai

credit card
kad kredit

breakfast
sarapan

lunch
makan tengah hari

dinner
makan malam

ticket
tiket

lift
lif

stamp
setem

border
sempadan

customs
kastam

embassy
kedutaan

visa
visa

passport
pasport

transport
pengangkutan

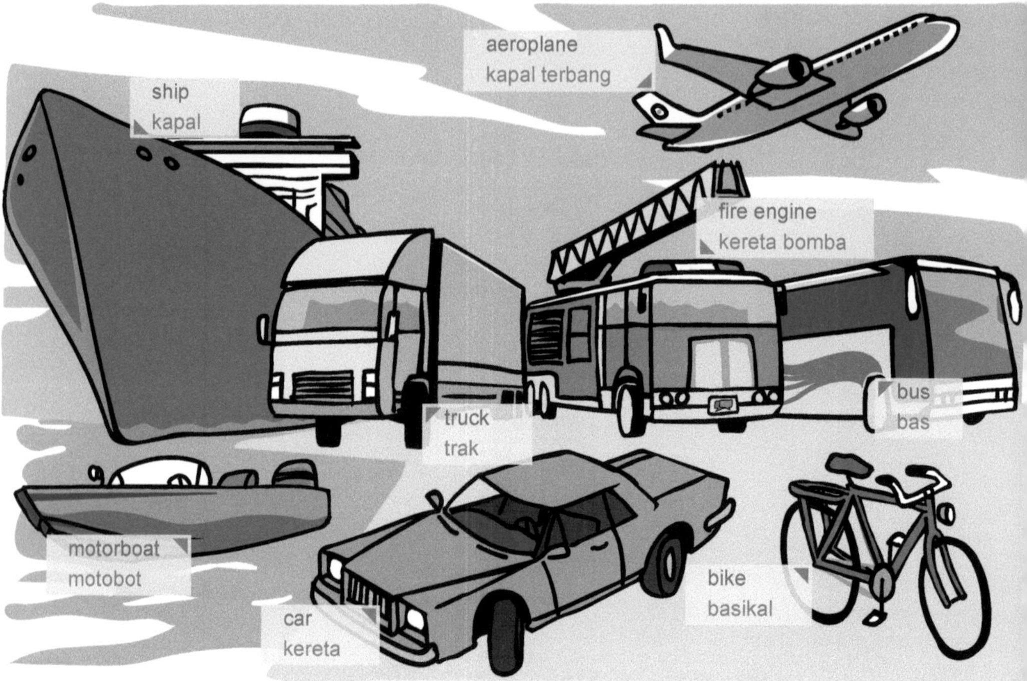

aeroplane
kapal terbang
ship
kapal
fire engine
kereta bomba
truck
trak
bus
bas
motorboat
motobot
bike
basikal
car
kereta

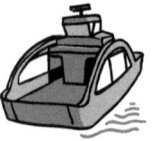

ferry

feri

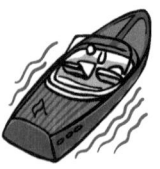

boat

bot

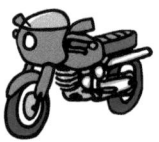

motorbike

motosikal

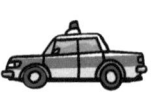

police car

kereta polis

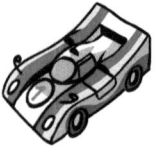

racing car

kereta lumba

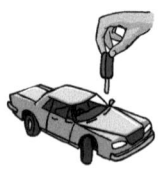

rental car

kereta sewa

car sharing

berkongsi kereta

breakdown truck

trak tunda

refuse truck

trak menolak

motor

motor

fuel

bahan api

petrol station

stesen minyak

traffic sign

tanda trafik

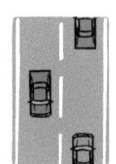

traffic

trafik

traffic jam

kesesakan lalu lintas

car park

tempat parkir

train station

stesen kereta api

tracks

trek

train

kereta api

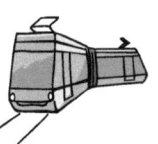

tram

trem

carriage

gerabak

helicopter

helikopter

airport

lapangan terbang

tower

Menara

passenger

penumpang

container

bekas

carton

kadbod

cart

kart

basket

bakul

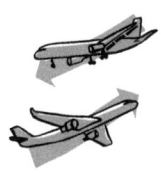

take off / land

berlepas / mendarat

city

bandar

village

kampung

city centre

pusat bandar

house

rumah

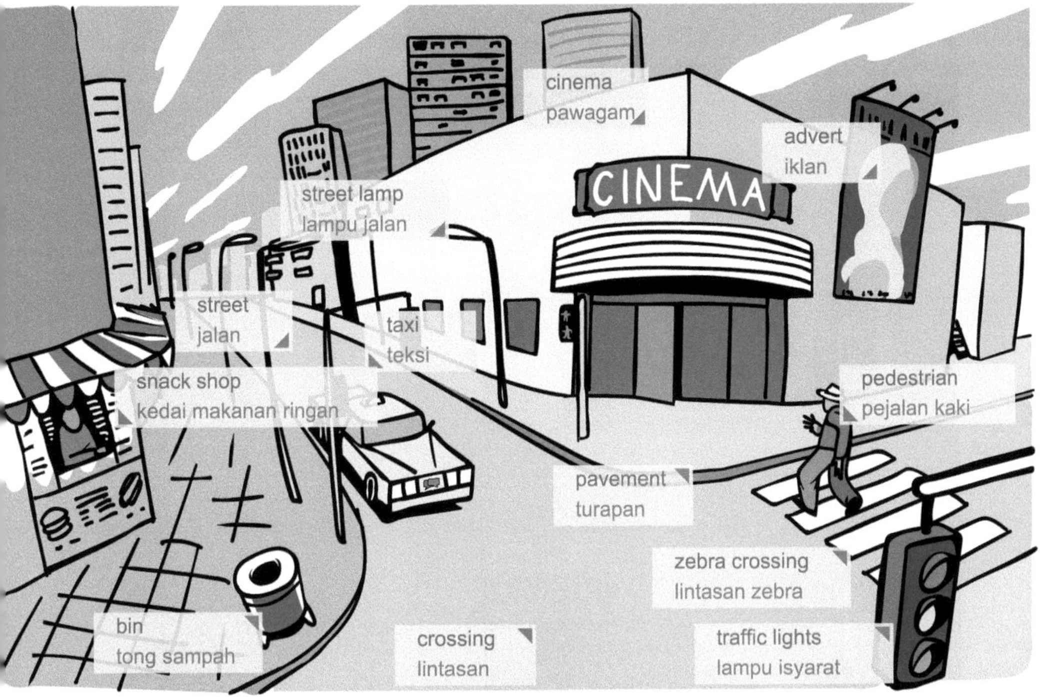

cinema
pawagam

advert
iklan

street lamp
lampu jalan

CINEMA

street
jalan

taxi
teksi

snack shop
kedai makanan ringan

pedestrian
pejalan kaki

pavement
turapan

zebra crossing
lintasan zebra

bin
tong sampah

crossing
lintasan

traffic lights
lampu isyarat

hut

pondok

flat

flat

train station

stesen kereta api

town hall

dewan bandar

museum

muzium

school

sekolah

city - bandar

university

universiti

bank

bank

hospital

hospital

hotel

hotel

pharmacy

farmasi

office

pejabat

book shop

kedai buku

shop

kedai

florist's

kedai bunga

supermarket

pasar raya

market

pasaran

department store

gedung

fishmonger's

penjual ikan

shopping centre

pusat membeli-belah

harbour

pelabuhan

park
taman

bench
bangku

bridge
jambatan

stairs
tangga

underground
bawah tanah

tunnel
terowong

bus stop
hentian bas

bar
bar

restaurant
restoran

postbox
peti surat

street sign
papan tanda jalan

parking meter
meter parkir

zoo
zoo

swimming pool
kolam renang

mosque
masjid

farm
ladang

pollution
pencemaran

graveyard
tanah perkuburan

church
gereja

playground
taman permainan

temple
kuil

landscape
landskap

signpost
tiang tanda

way
jalan

meadow
padang rumput

stone
batu

tree
pokok

hiker
pejalan kaki

river
sungai

grass
rumput

flower
bunga

valley

lembah

hill

bukit

lake

tasik

forest

hutan

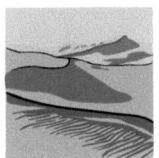

desert

padang pasir

volcano

gunung berapi

castle

istana

rainbow

pelangi

mushroom

cendawan

palm tree

pokok kelapa sawit

mosquito

nyamuk

fly

terbang

ant

semut

bee

lebah

spider

labah-labah

beetle

kumbang

frog

katak

squirrel

tupai

hedgehog

landak

hare

arnab

owl

burung hantu

bird

burung

swan

angsa

boar

babi jantan

deer

rusa

moose

moose

dam

empangan

wind turbine

turbin angin

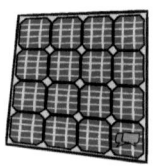

solar panel

panel solar

climate

iklim

restaurant

restoran

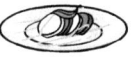

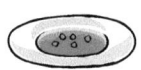

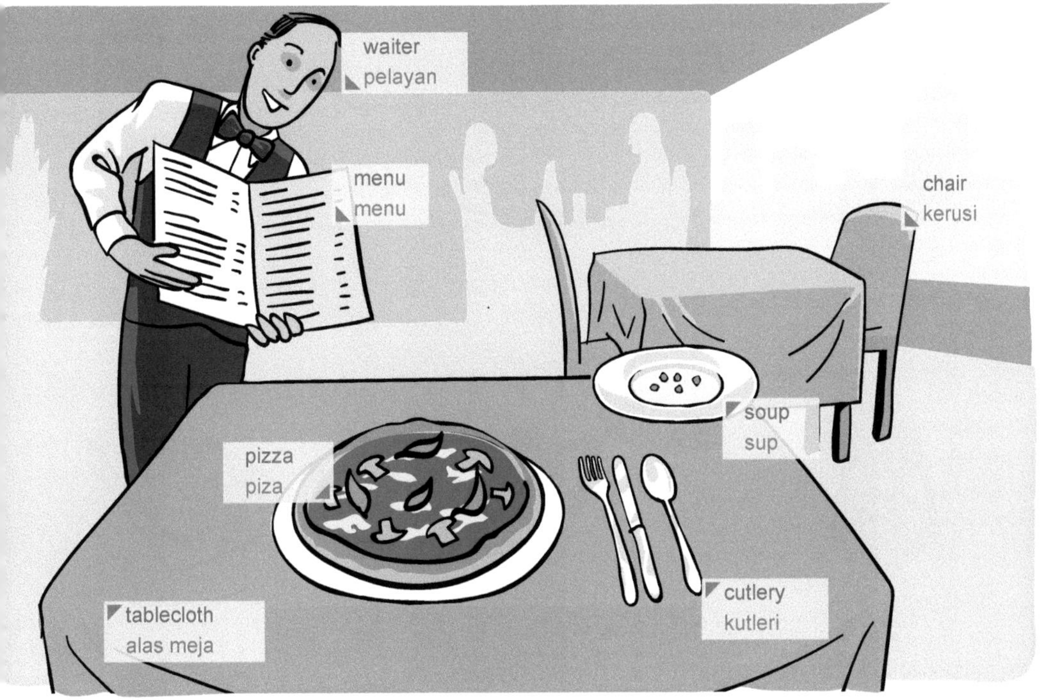
waiter
pelayan
menu
menu
chair
kerusi
soup
sup
pizza
piza
cutlery
kutleri
tablecloth
alas meja

starter
pemula

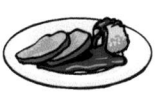

main course
hidangan utama

dessert
pencuci mulut

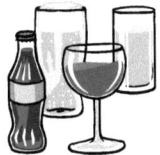

drinks
minuman

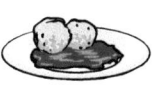

food
makanan

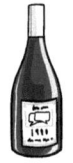

bottle
botol

fast food

makanan segera

street food

makanan jalanan

teapot

teko

sugar bowl

mangkuk gula

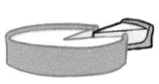

portion

bahagian

espresso machine

mesin espreso

high chair

kerusi tinggi

bill

bil

tray

dulang

knife

pisau

fork

garfu

spoon

sudu

teaspoon

sudu teh

serviette

serviette

glass

gelas

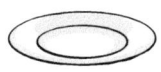

plate

pinggan

soup plate

mangkuk sup

saucer

piring

sauce

sos

salt pot

tempat garam

pepper mill

pengisar lada

vinegar

cuka

oil

minyak

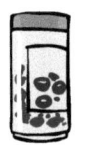

spices

rempah

ketchup

sos

mustard

mustard

mayonnaise

mayones

supermarket

pasar raya

special offer
tawaran istimewa
FOR
customer
pelanggan
dairy
tenusu
fruit
buah-buahan
trolley
troli

BUTCHERS

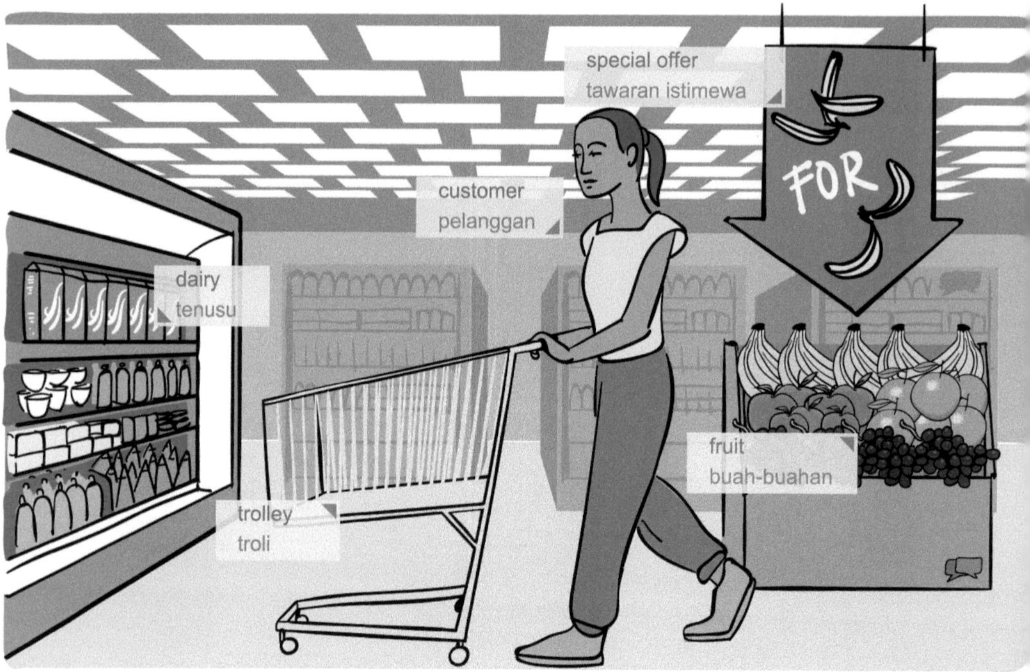

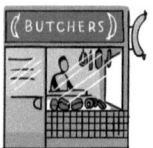

butcher´s

tukang daging

BAKERY

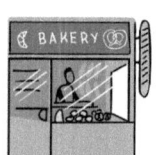

baker´s

kedai roti

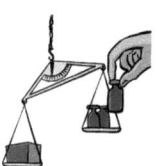

weigh

berat

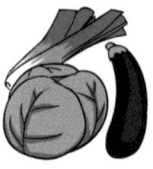

vegetables

sayur-sayuran

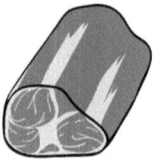

meat

daging

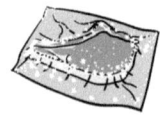

frozen food

makanan sejuk beku

cold meat

daging sejuk

tinned food

makanan dalam tin

washing powder

serbuk pencuci

sweets

gula-gula

household products

produk isi rumah

cleaning products

produk pembersihan

salesperson

orang jualan

till

daftar tunai

cashier

juruwang

shopping list

senarai membeli-belah

opening hours

waktu pembukaan

wallet

beg duit

credit card

kad kredit

bag

beg

plastic bag

beg plastik

water
....
air

juice
....
jus

milk
....
susu

coke
....
kola

wine
....
wain

beer
....
bir

alcohol
....
alkohol

cocoa
....
koko

tea
....
the

coffee
....
kopi

espresso
....
espreso

cappuccino
....
kapucino

banana

pisang

apple

epal

orange

oren

melon

tembikai

lemon

lemon

carrot

lobak merah

garlic

bawang putih

bamboo

buluh

onion

bawang

mushroom

cendawan

nuts

kacang

noodles

mi

spaghetti

spageti

rice

nasi

salad

salad

chips

kerepek

fried potatoes

kentang goreng

pizza

piza

hamburger

hamburger

sandwich

sandwic

cutlet

kutlet

ham

ham

salami

salami

sausage

sosej

chicken

ayam

roast

panggang

fish

ikan

porridge oats

bubur oat

muesli

muesli

cornflakes

emping jagung

flour

tepung

croissant

kroisan

bread roll

roti roll

bread

roti

toast

roti bakar

biscuits

biskut

butter

mentega

curd

dadih

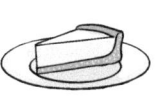

cake

kek

egg

telur

fried egg

telur goreng

cheese

keju

ice cream

ais krim

sugar

gula

honey

madu

jam

jem

chocolate spread

krim nougat

curry

kari

food - makanan

goat

kambing

cow

lembu

calf

anak lembu

pig

babi

piglet

anak babi

bull

lembu

goose

angsa

duck

itik

chick

anak ayam

hen

ayam betina

cock

ayam jantan muda

rat

tikus

cat

kucing

mouse

tikus

ox

lembu jantan

dog

anjing

doghouse

rumah anjing

garden hose

hos taman

watering can

bekas siraman

scythe

sabit

plough

bajak

sickle

sabit

hoe

cangkul

pitchfork

serampang peladang

axe

kapak

wheelbarrow

kereta sorong

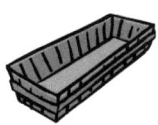

trough

palung

milk can

tin susu

sack

karung

fence

pagar

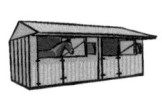

stable

stabil

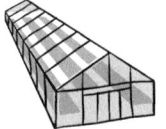

greenhouse

rumah hijau

soil

tanah

seed

benih

fertilizer

baja

combine harvester

jentuai

harvest

tuai

harvest

menuai

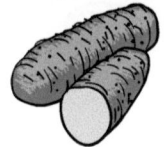

yams

keladi

wheat

gandum

soy

soya

potato

kentang

corn

jagung

rapeseed

biji sawi

fruit tree

pokok buah-buahan

cassava

ubi kayu

cereals

bijirin

house
rumah

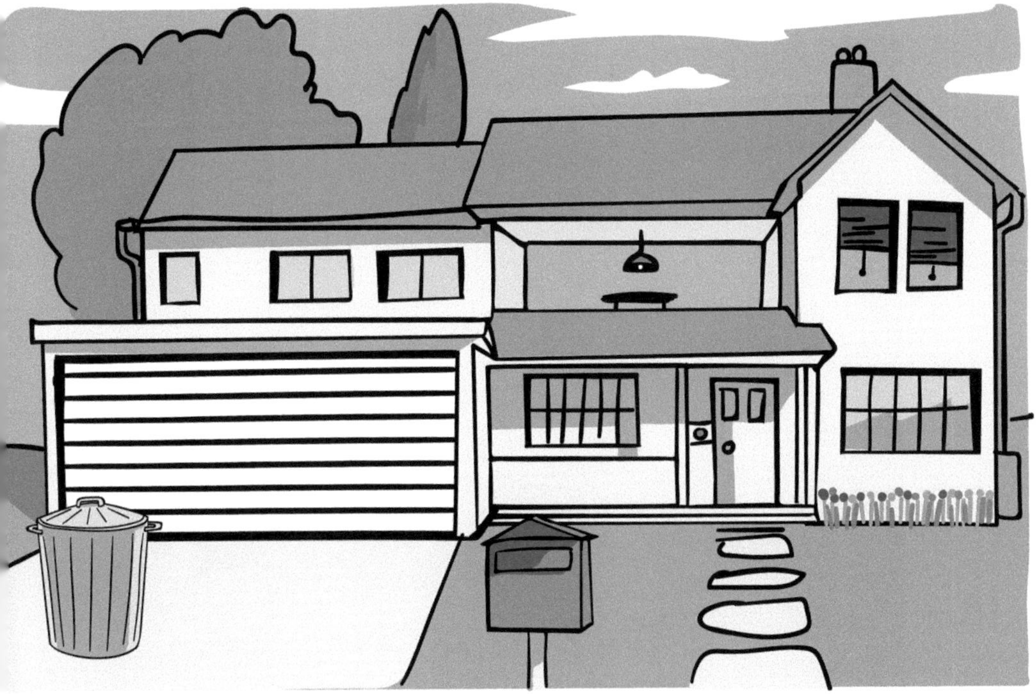

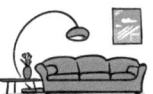

living room
ruang tamu

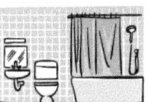

bathroom
bilik air

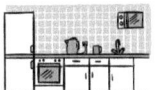

kitchen
dapur

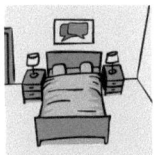

bedroom
bilik tidur

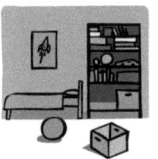

child's room
bilik kanak-kanak

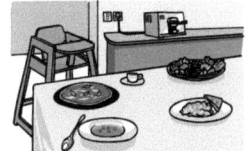

dining room
ruang makan

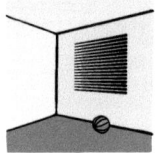

floor

lantai

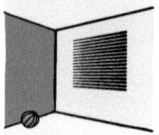

wall

dinding

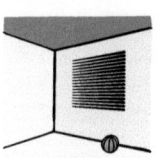

ceiling

siling

cellar

bilik bawah tanah

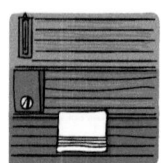

sauna

sauna

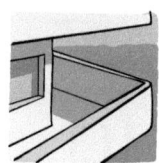

balcony

balkoni

terrace

teres

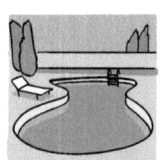

pool

kolam renang

lawn mower

pemotong rumput

sheet

lembaran

bedspread

penutup tilam

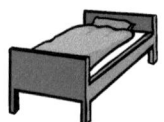

bed

katil

broom

penyapu

bucket

timba

switch

suis

living room
ruang tamu

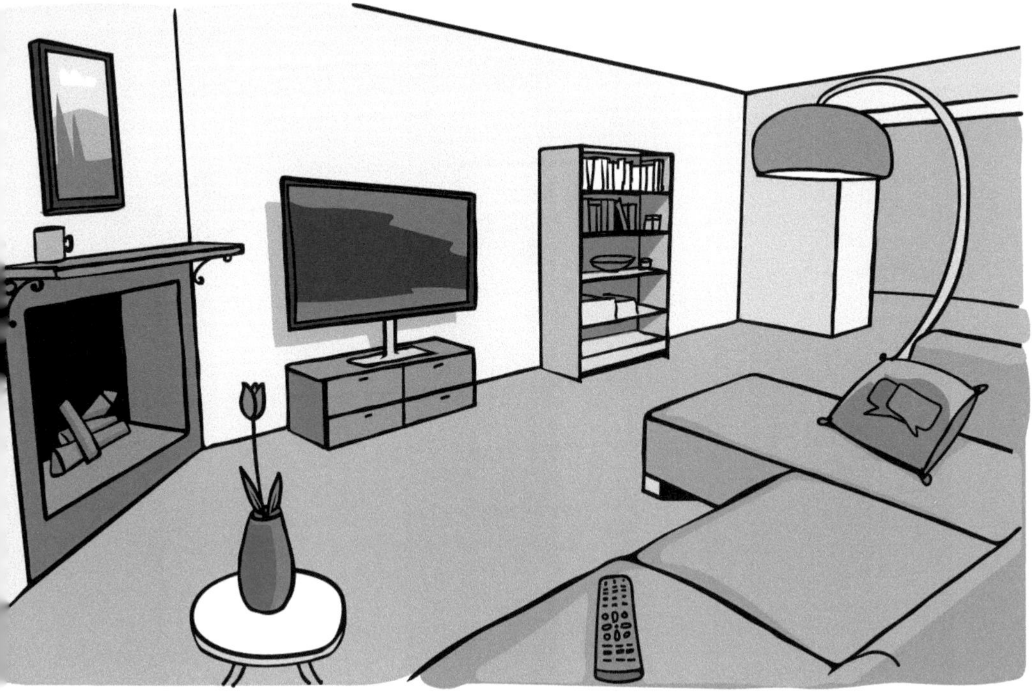

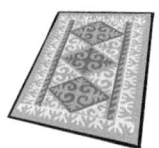

carpet
permaidani

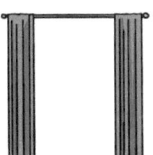

curtain
tirai

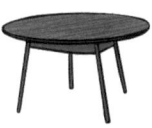

table
meja

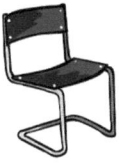

chair
kerusi

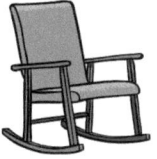

rocking chair
kerusi malas

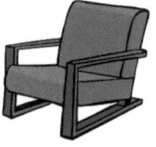

armchair
kerusi

book

buku

blanket

selimut

decoration

hiasan

firewood

kayu api

film

filem

hi-fi equipment

hi-fi

key

kunci

newspaper

akhbar

painting

lukisan

poster

poster

radio

radio

notepad

buku catatan

hoover

penyedut habuk

cactus

kaktus

candle

lilin

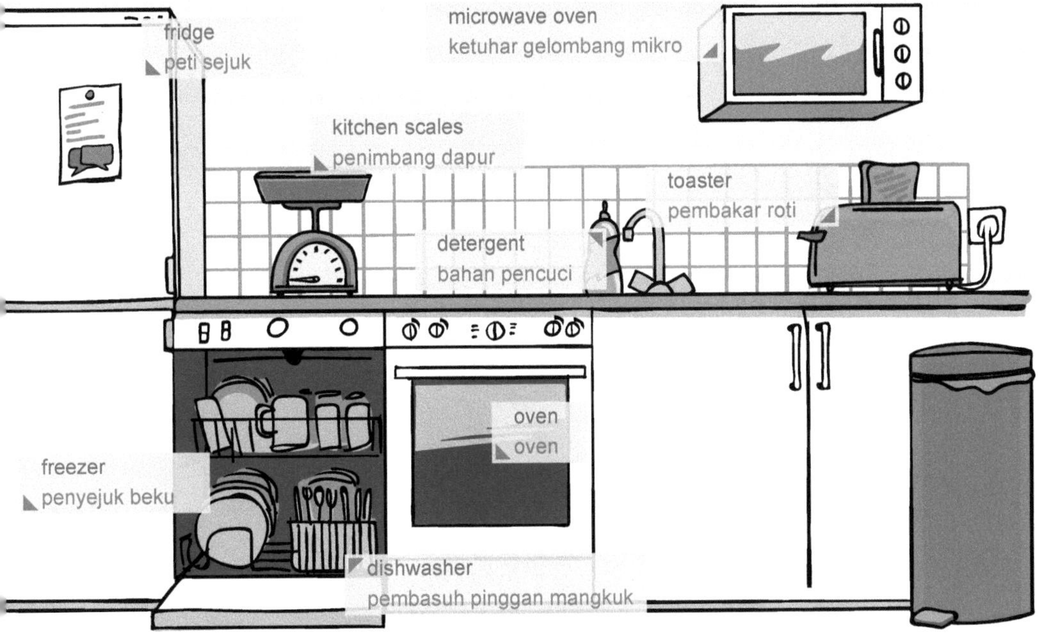

fridge
peti sejuk

microwave oven
ketuhar gelombang mikro

kitchen scales
penimbang dapur

toaster
pembakar roti

detergent
bahan pencuci

oven
oven

freezer
penyejuk beku

dishwasher
pembasuh pinggan mangkuk

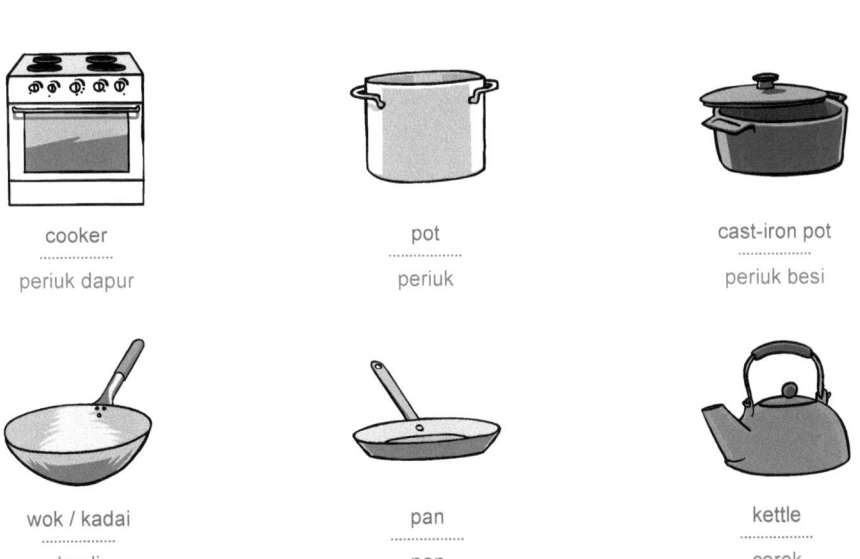

cooker	pot	cast-iron pot
periuk dapur	periuk	periuk besi
wok / kadai	pan	kettle
kuali	pan	cerek

steamer

pengukus

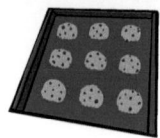

baking tray

dulang pembakar

crockery

pinggan mangkuk

mug

koleh

bowl

mangkuk

chopsticks

penyepit

ladle

senduk

spatula

spatula

whisk

pengadun

strainer

penapis

sieve

ayak

grater

pemarut

mortar

mortar

barbecue

barbeku

open fire

pembakaran terbuka

chopping board

papan pencincang

rolling pin

pin golekan

corkscrew

skru gabus

can

tin

can opener

pembuka tin

pot holder

pemegang periuk

sink

sinki

brush

berus

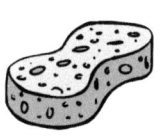

sponge

span

blender

pengisar

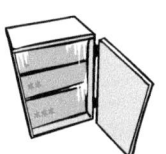

deep freezer

penyejuk beku

baby bottle

botol bayi

tap

paip

bathroom
bilik air

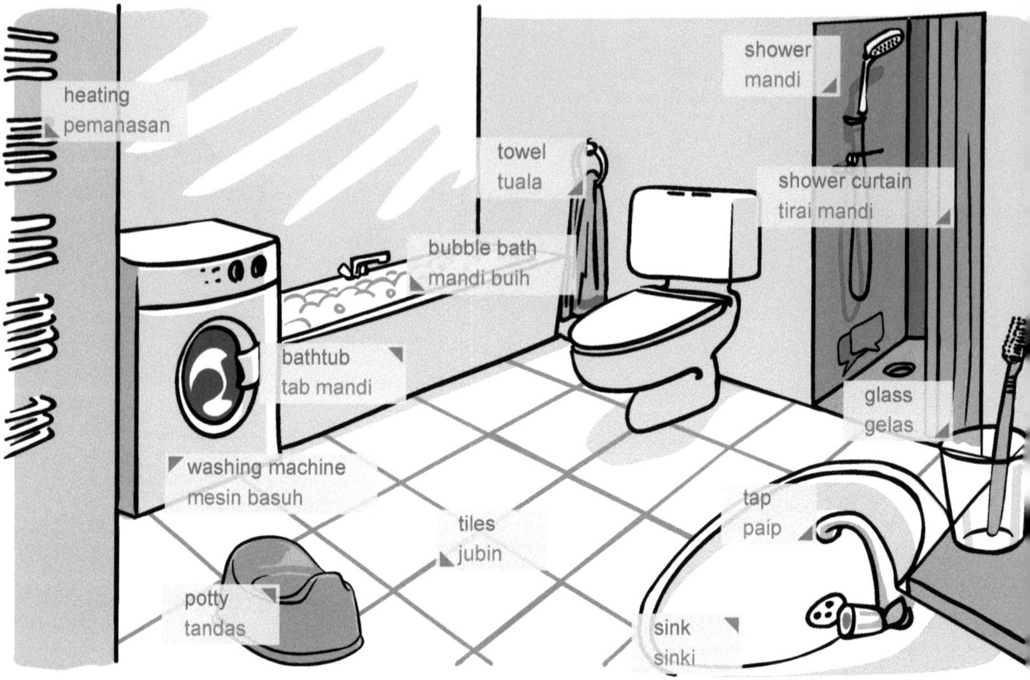
heating
pemanasan
shower
mandi
towel
tuala
shower curtain
tirai mandi
bubble bath
mandi buih
bathtub
tab mandi
glass
gelas
washing machine
mesin basuh
tap
paip
tiles
jubin
potty
tandas
sink
sinki

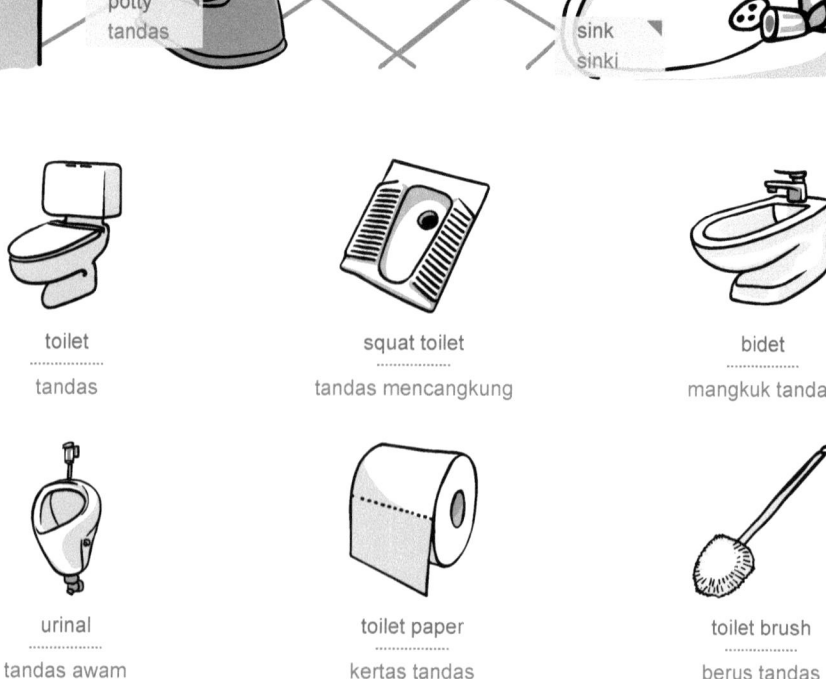

toilet

tandas

squat toilet

tandas mencangkung

bidet

mangkuk tandas

urinal

tandas awam

toilet paper

kertas tandas

toilet brush

berus tandas

toothbrush

berus gigi

toothpaste

ubat gigi

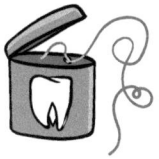

dental floss

flos gigi

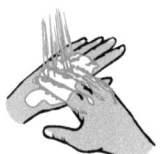

wash

cuci

handheld shower

mandian tangan

douche

pancuran

basin

besen

back brush

belakang berus

soap

sabun

shower gel

gel mandian

shampoo

syampu

flannel

flanel

drain

longkang

cream

krim

deodorant

deodoran

mirror

cermin

hand mirror

cermin tangan

razor

pisau cukur

shaving foam

busa cukur

aftershave

selepas cukur

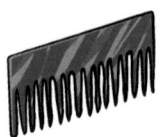

comb

sikat

brush

berus

hair dryer

pengering rambut

hairspray

semburan rambut

makeup

mekap

lipstick

gincu

nail varnish

varnis kuku

cotton wool

bulu kapas

nail scissors

gunting kuku

perfume

pewangi

washbag

beg basuhan

stool

bangku

weighing scale

skala berat

bathrobe

jubah mandi

rubber gloves

sarung tangan getah

tampon

kapas

sanitary towel

tuala wanita

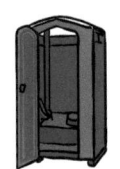

chemical toilet

tandas kimia

child's room
bilik kanak-kanak

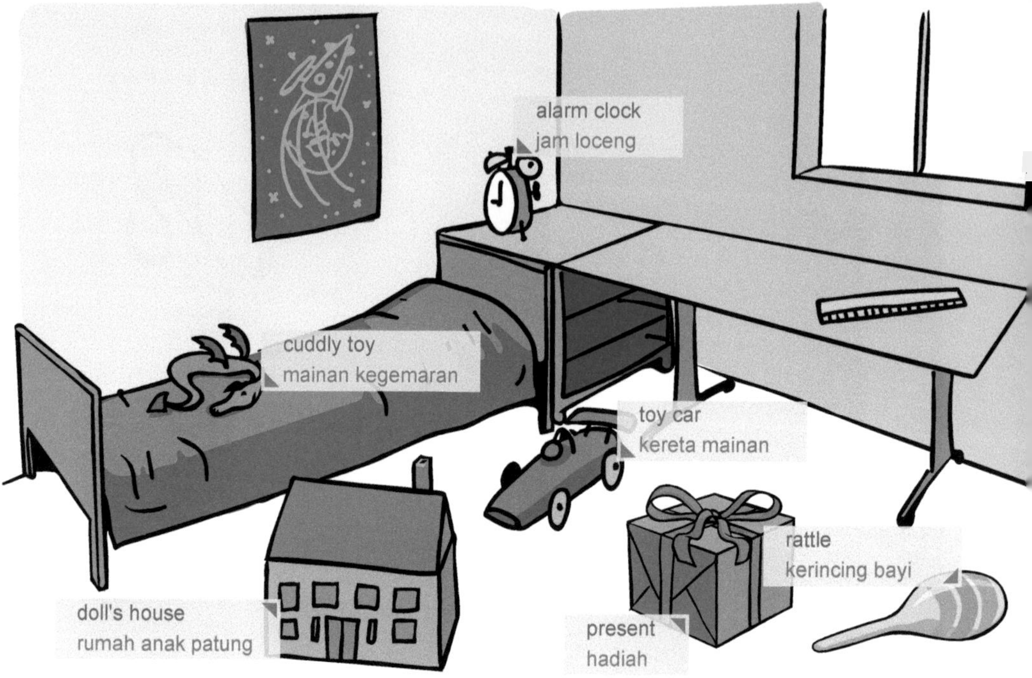
alarm clock
jam loceng
cuddly toy
mainan kegemaran
toy car
kereta mainan
rattle
kerincing bayi
doll's house
rumah anak patung
present
hadiah

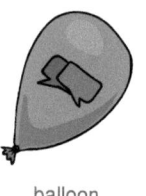

balloon
belon

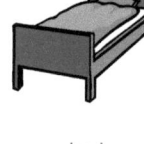

bed
katil

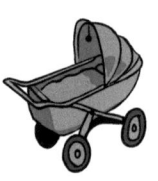

pram
kereta sorong bayi

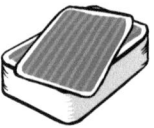

deck of cards
set kad

jigsaw
susun suai gambar

SUPER MEGA

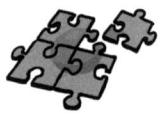

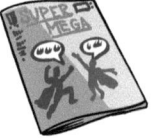

comic
komik

lego bricks

batu bata lego

building blocks

blok mainan

action figure

figura aksi

babygrow

baju bayi

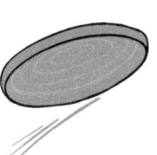

frisbee

frisbee

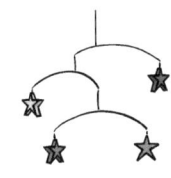

mobile

mainan bayi mudah alih

board game

permainan papan

dice

dadu

model train set

set model kereta api

dummy

palsu

party

parti

picture book

buku bergambar

ball

bola

doll

anak patung

play

main

sandpit

lubang pasir

swing

buai

toys

mainan

video game console

konsol permainan video

tricycle

basikal roda tiga

teddy bear

anak patung beruang

wardrobe

almari pakaian

clothing

pakaian

socks

stoking

stockings

stoking

tights

ketat

scarf
skarf

umbrella
payung

t-shirt
kemeja-t

keselamatan

boots
but

slippers
selipar

trainers
kasut sukan

sandals
sandal

shoes
kasut

rubber boots
but getah

underpants
seluar dalam

bra
coli

vest
ves

clothing - pakaian

45

body

badan

trousers

Seluar panjang

jeans

jean

skirt

skirt

blouse

blaus

shirt

kemeja

pullover

baju panas sarung

hoodie

sweater

blazer

blazer

jacket

jaket

coat

kot

raincoat

baju hujan

costume

kostum

dress

pakaian

wedding dress

baju pengantin

suit

sut

nightgown

baju tidur

pyjamas

baju tidur

sari

sari

headscarf

skarf kepala

turban

serban

burqa

burqa

kaftan

kaftan

abaya

abaya/jubah

swimsuit

baju renang

trunks

seluar renang

shorts

seluar pendek

tracksuit

sut balapan

apron

apron

gloves

sarung tangan

button

butang

glasses

cermin mata

bracelet

gelang tangan

necklace

rantai leher

ring

cincin

earring

subang

cap

topi

coat hanger

penyangkut kot

hat

topi

tie

tali leher

zip

zip

helmet

topi keledar

braces

pendakap

school uniform

uniform sekolah

uniform

seragam

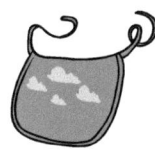

bib

lapik dada

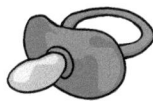

dummy

palsu

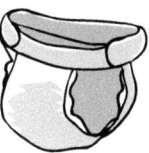

nappy

lampin

office

pejabat

server
pelayan
filing cabinet
kabinet fail
printer
mesin pencetak
paper
kertas
monitor
monitor
mouse
tetikus
desk
meja
folder
folder
keyboard
papan kekunci
waste-paper basket
bakul sampah
computer
komputer
chair
kerusi

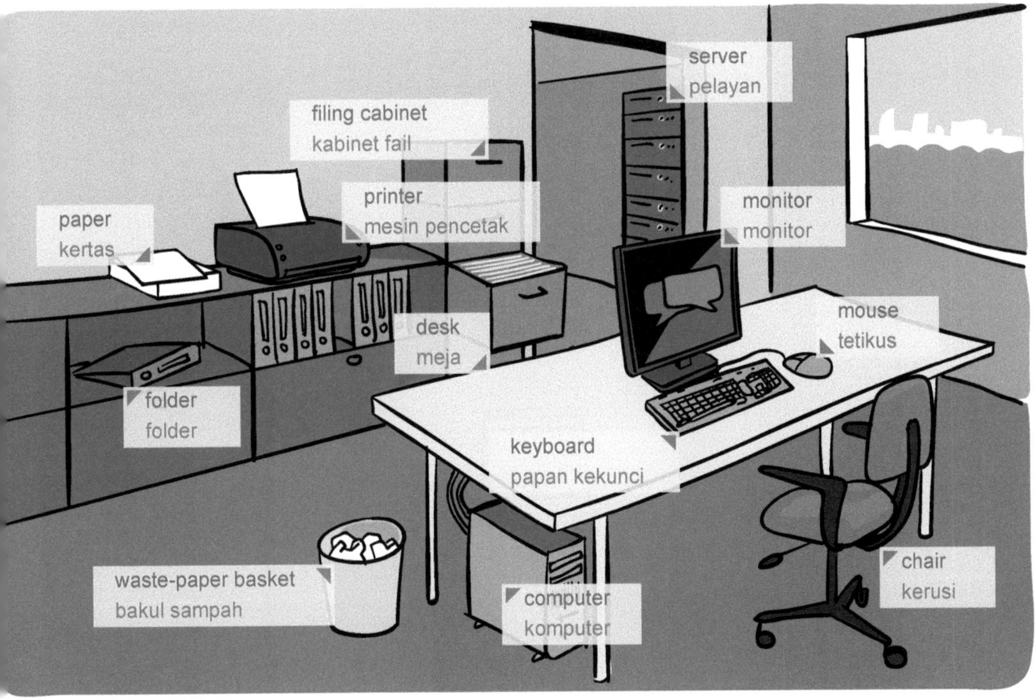

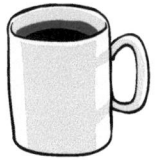

coffee mug

cawan kopi

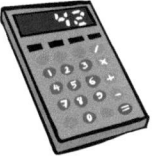

calculator

kalkulator

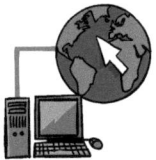

internet

internet

laptop

komputer riba

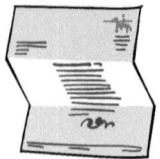

letter

surat

message

mesej

mobile

mudah alih

network

rangkaian

photocopier

mesin fotokopi

software

perisian

telephone

telefon

plug socket

soket plag

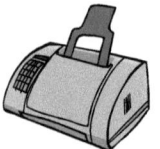

fax machine

mesin faks

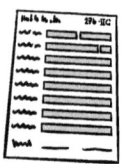

form

bentuk

document

dokumen

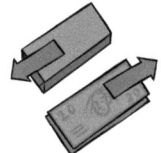

buy

beli

pay

bayar

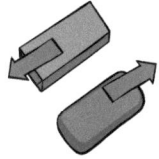

trade

berdagang

money

wang

 **USD**

dollar

dolar

 **EUR**

euro

euro

 **JPY**

yen

yen

 **RUB**

rouble

rubel

 **CHF**

Swiss franc

franc swiss

 **CNY**

renminbi yuan

renminbi yuan

 **INR**

rupee

rupee

cashpoint

mata tunai

bureau de change

pejabat tukaran mata wang

gold

emas

silver

perak

oil

minyak

energy

tenaga

price

harga

contract

kontrak

tax

cukai

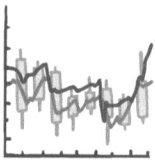

stock

stok

work

kerja

employee

pekerja

employer

majikan

factory

kilang

shop

kedai

economy - ekonomi

occupations
pekerjaan

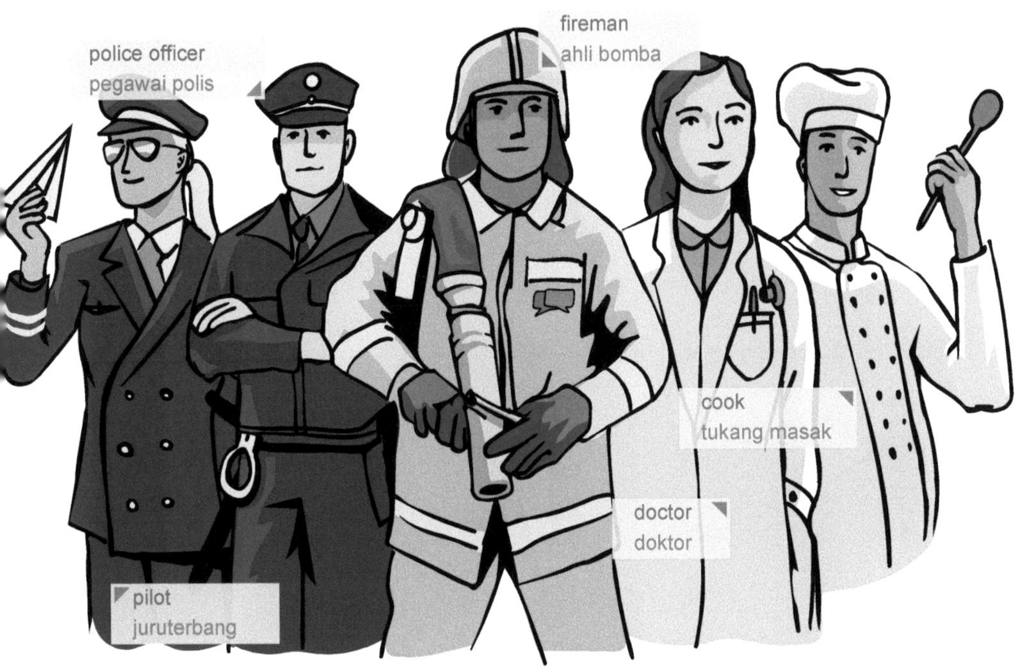

police officer
pegawai polis
fireman
ahli bomba
cook
tukang masak
doctor
doktor
pilot
juruterbang

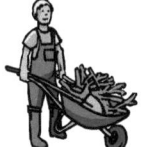

gardener

tukang kebun

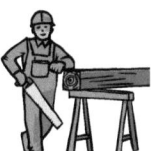

carpenter

tukang kayu

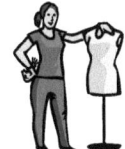

seamstress

tukang jahit

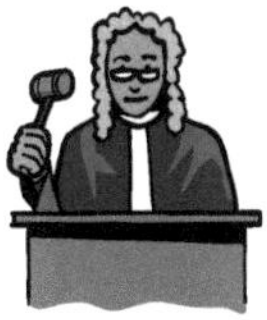

judge

hakim

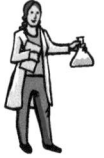

chemist

ahli kimia

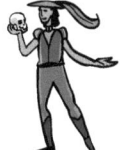

actor

pelakon

bus driver

pemandu bas

taxi driver

pemandu teksi

fisherman

nelayan

cleaning lady

wanita pencuci

roofer

kasau

waiter

pelayan

hunter

pemburu

painter

pelukis

baker

bakeri

electrician

juruelektrik

builder

pembangun

engineer

jurutera

butcher

penjual daging

plumber

tukang paip

postman

posmen

soldier

askar

architect

arkitek

cashier

juruwang

florist

kedai bunga

hairdresser

pendandan rambut

conductor

konduktor

mechanic

mekanik

captain

kapten

dentist

doktor gigi

scientist

ahli sains

rabbi

tuhanku

imam

imam

monk

sami

clergyman

paderi

tools
alat

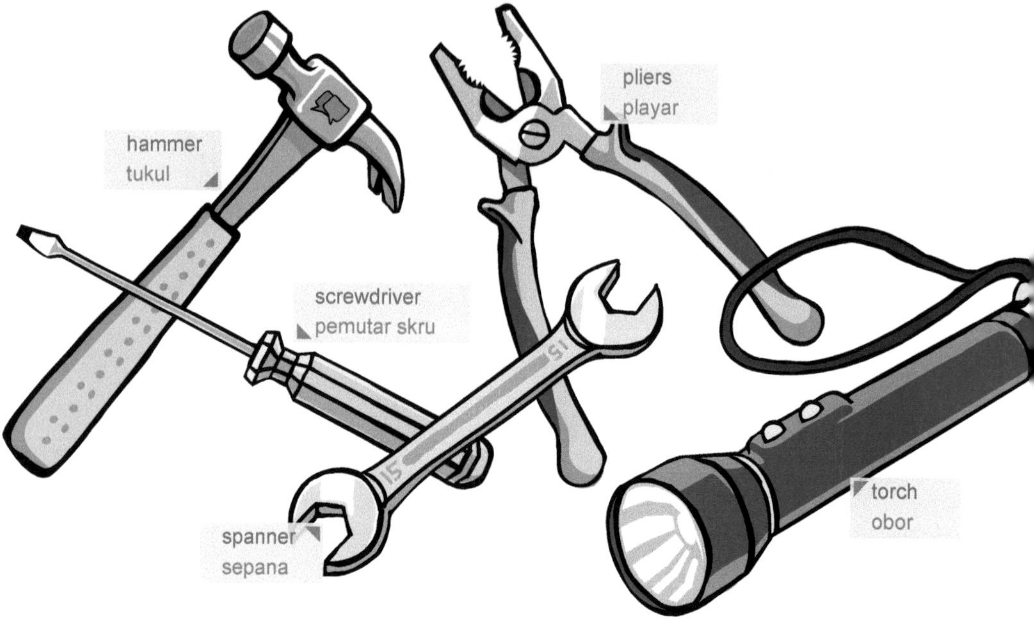

hammer
tukul
pliers
playar
screwdriver
pemutar skru
spanner
sepana
torch
obor

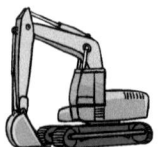

digger
pengorek

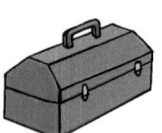

toolbox
kotak peralatan

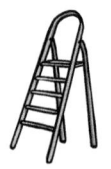

ladder
tangga

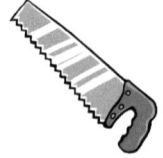

saw
gergaji

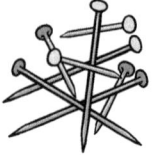

nails
kuku

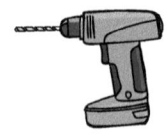

drill
gerudi

repair

baiki

shovel

penyodok

Damn!

Celaka!

dustpan

penadah sampah

paint pot

periuk cat

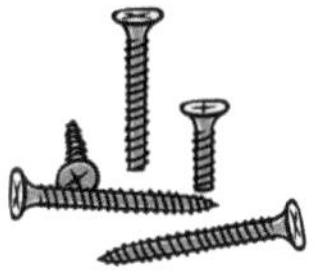

screws

skru

musical instruments
alat muzik

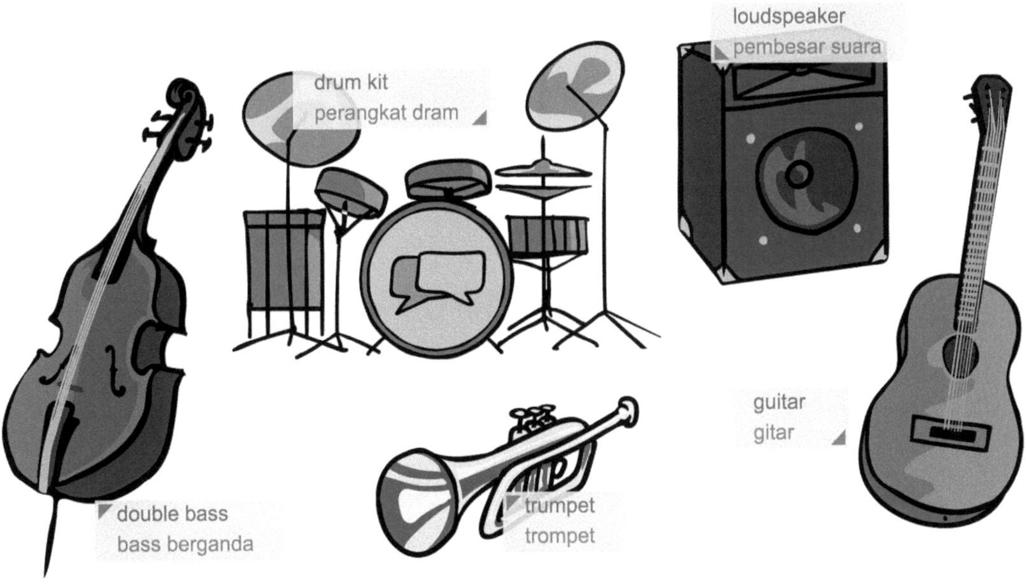

loudspeaker
pembesar suara

drum kit
perangkat dram

guitar
gitar

double bass
bass berganda

trumpet
trompet

piano

piano

violin

biola

bass

bass

timpani

timpani

drums

dram

keyboard

papan kekunci

saxophone

saksofon

flute

seruling

microphone

mikrofon

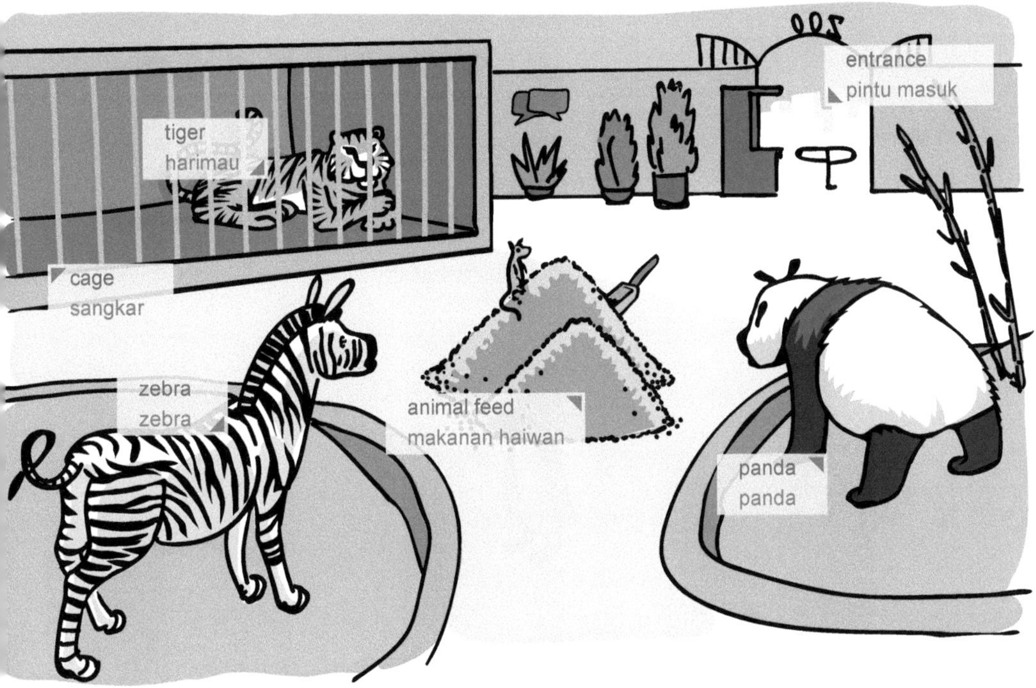

tiger
harimau

cage
sangkar

zebra
zebra

animal feed
makanan haiwan

entrance
pintu masuk

panda
panda

animals

haiwan

elephant

gajah

kangaroo

kanggaru

rhino

badak sumbu

gorilla

gorila

bear

beruang

camel

unta

ostrich

burung unta

lion

singa

monkey

monyet

flamingo

flamingo

parrot

nuri

polar bear

beruang kutub

penguin

penguin

shark

yu

peacock

merak

snake

ular

crocodile

buaya

zookeeper

penjaga zoo

seal

anjing laut

jaguar

jaguar

pony

kuda

leopard

harimau

hippo

badak air

giraffe

zirafah

eagle

helang

boar

babi jantan

fish

ikan

turtle

penyu

walrus

anjing laut

fox

musang

gazelle

rusa

American football
bola sepak Amerika

cycling
berbasikal

tennis
tenis

basketball
bola keranjang

swimming
renang

boxing
tinju

ice hockey
hoki ais

football
bola sepak

badminton
badminton

athletics
olahraga

handball
bola baling

skiing
ski

polo
polo

jump
lompat

laugh
ketawa

hug
peluk

walk
berjalan

sing
menyanyi

dream
mimpi

pray
berdoa

kiss
cium

write	draw	show
tulis	lukis	tunjuk

push	give	take
tolak	beri	ambil

have
....
ada

do
....
buat

be
....
ialah

stand
....
berdiri

run
....
lari

pull
....
tarik

throw
....
buang

fall
....
jatuh

lie
....
tipu

wait
....
tunggu

carry
....
bawa

sit
....
duduk

get dressed
....
pakai

sleep
....
tidur

wake up
....
bangkit

look at

lihat pada

cry

menangis

stroke

strok

comb

sikat

talk

cakap

understand

faham

ask

tanya

listen

dengar

drink

minum

eat

makan

tidy up

mengemas

love

sayang

cook

masak

drive

pandu

fly

terbang

sail

belayar

calculate

kira

read

baca

learn

belajar

work

kerja

marry

nikah

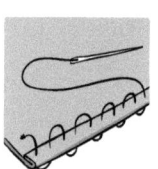

sew

jahit

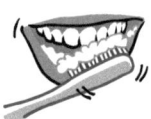

brush teeth

memberus gigi

kill

bunuh

smoke

asap

send

hantar

family
keluarga

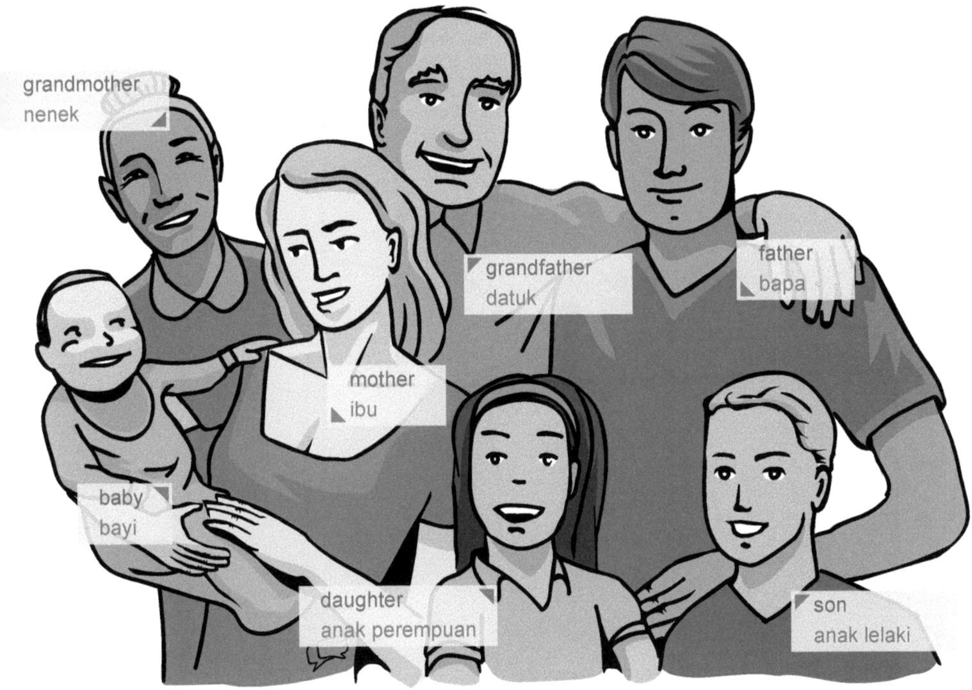
grandmother
nenek
grandfather
datuk
father
bapa
mother
ibu
baby
bayi
daughter
anak perempuan
son
anak lelaki

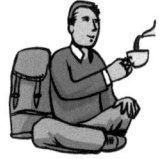

guest
tetamu

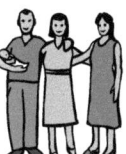

aunt
mak cik

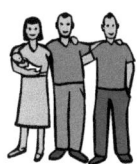

uncle
pak cik

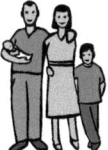

brother
abang

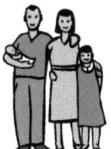

sister
kakak

body
badan

forehead
dahi
eye
mata
shoulder
bahu
finger
jari
face
muka
chin
dagu
hand
tangan
leg
kaki
breast
dada
arm
lengan

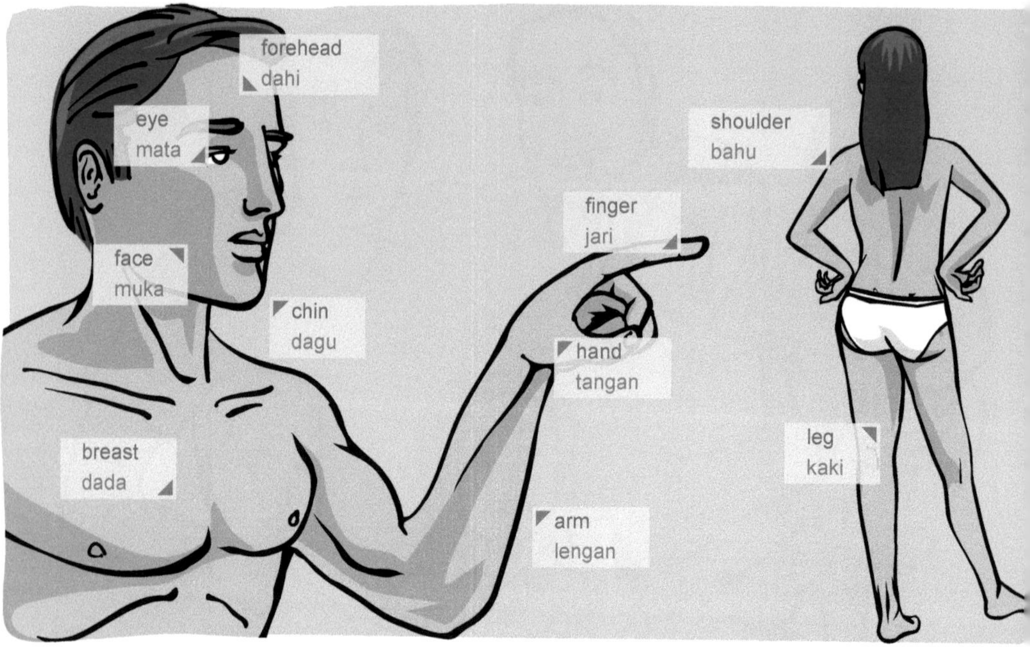

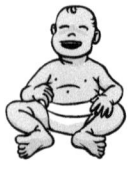

baby

bayi

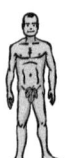

man

lelaki

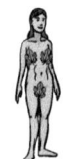

woman

wanita

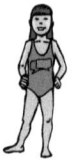

girl

perempuan

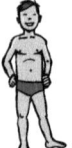

boy

lelaki

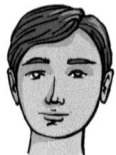

head

kepala

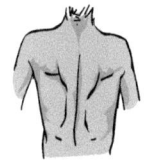

back

belakang

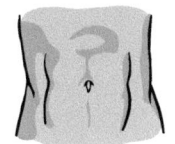

belly

bawah perut

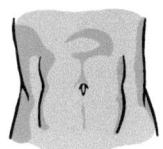

belly button

pusat

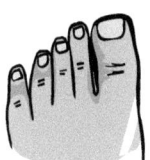

toe

jari kaki

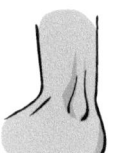

heel

tumit

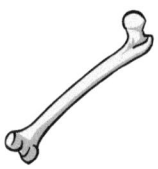

bone

tulang

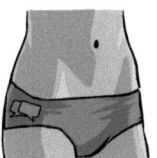

hip

pinggul

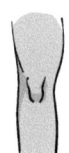

knee

lutut

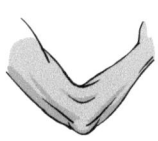

elbow

siku

nose

hidung

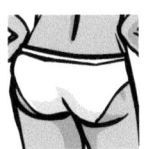

bottom

bawah

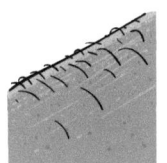

skin

kulit

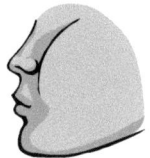

cheek

pipi

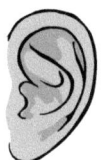

ear

telinga

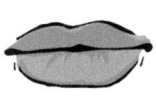

lip

bibir

mouth

mulut

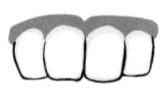

tooth

gigi

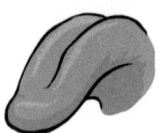

tongue

lidah

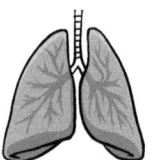

brain

otak

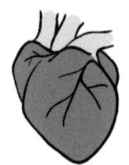

heart

hati

muscle

otot

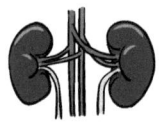

lung

paru-paru

liver

hati

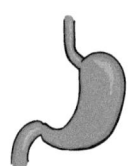

stomach

perut

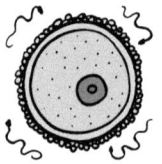

kidneys

buah pinggang

sex

seks

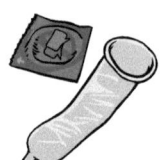

condom

kondom

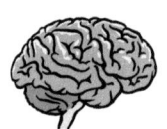

ovum

faraj

semen

mani

pregnancy

mengandung

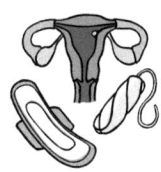

menstruation
haid

vagina
faraj

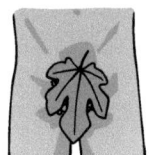

penis
penis

eyebrow
kening

hair
rambut

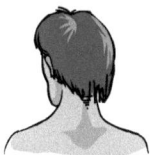

neck
leher

hospital
hospital

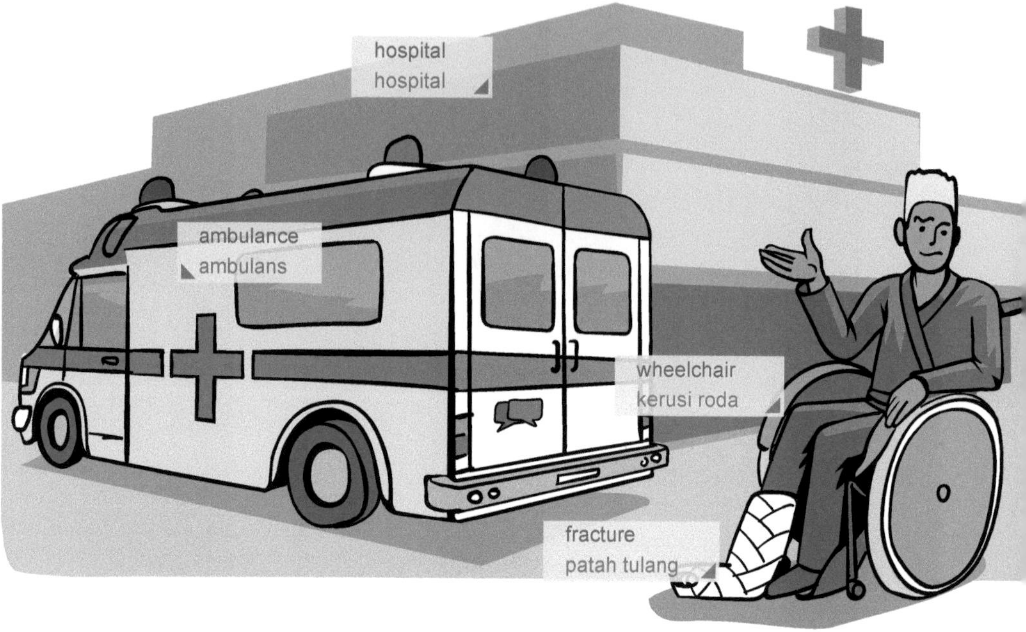

hospital
hospital
ambulance
ambulans
wheelchair
kerusi roda
fracture
patah tulang

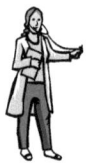

doctor

doktor

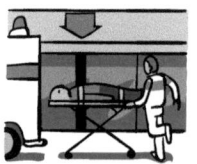

emergency room

bilik kecemasan

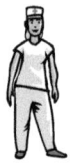

nurse

jururawat

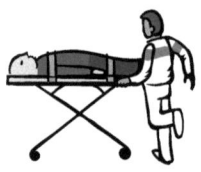

emergency

kecemasan

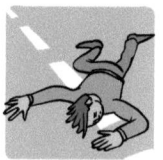

unconscious

tak sedar

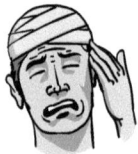

pain

sakit

injury

kecederaan

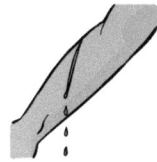

bleeding

pendarahan

heart attack

serangan jantung

stroke

strok

allergy

alergi

cough

batuk

fever

demam

flu

selesema

diarrhoea

cirit-birit

headache

sakit kepala

cancer

kanser

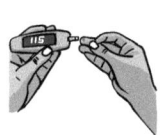

diabetes

diabetes

surgeon

pakar bedah

scalpel

pisau bedah

operation

pembedahan

CT

CT

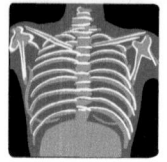

x-ray

x-ray

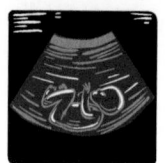

ultrasound

ultrabunyi

face mask

topeng muka

disease

penyakit

waiting room

bilik menunggu

crutch

penongkat

plaster

plaster

bandage

pembalut

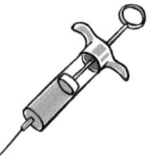

injection

suntikan

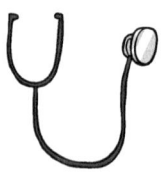

stethoscope

stetoskop

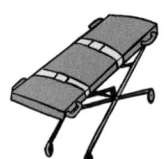

stretcher

pengusung

clinical thermometer

termometer klinik

birth

kelahiran

overweight

berat badan berlebihan

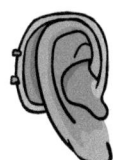

hearing aid

alat pendengaran

disinfectant

disinfektan

infection

jangkitan

virus

virus

HIV / AIDS

HIV / AIDS

medicine

perubatan

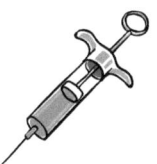

vaccination

vaksinasi

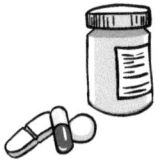

tablets

tablet

pill

pil

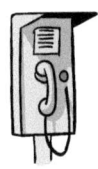

emergency call

panggilan kecemasan

blood pressure monitor

pantau tekanan darah

ill / healthy

sakit / sihat

Help!

Tolong!

alarm

penggera

assault

serang

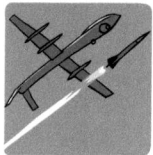

attack

serangan

danger

bahaya

emergency exit

pintu kecemasan

Fire!

Api!

fire extinguisher

alat pemadam api

accident

kemalangan

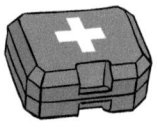

first-aid kit

alat pertolongan cemas

SOS

SOS

police

polis

Europe

Eropah

North America

Amerika Utara

South America

Amerika Selatan

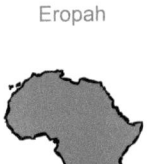

Africa

Afrika

Asia

Asia

Australia

Australia

Atlantic

Atlantic

Pacific

Pasifik

Indian Ocean

Lautan Hindi

Antarctic Ocean

Lautan Antartik

Arctic Ocean

Lautan Artik

North Pole

Kutub utara

South Pole

Kutub Selatan

Antarctica

Antartika

Earth

bumi

land

tanah

sea

laut

island

pulau

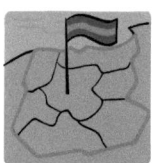

nation

negara

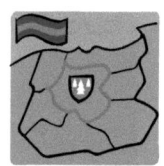

state

negeri

clock face
....
muka jam

hour hand
....
tangan jam

minute hand
....
tangan minit

second hand
....
terpakai

What time is it?
....
Jam berapa sekarang

day
....
hari

time
....
masa

now
....
sekarang

digital watch
....
jam digital

minute
....
minit

hour
....
jam

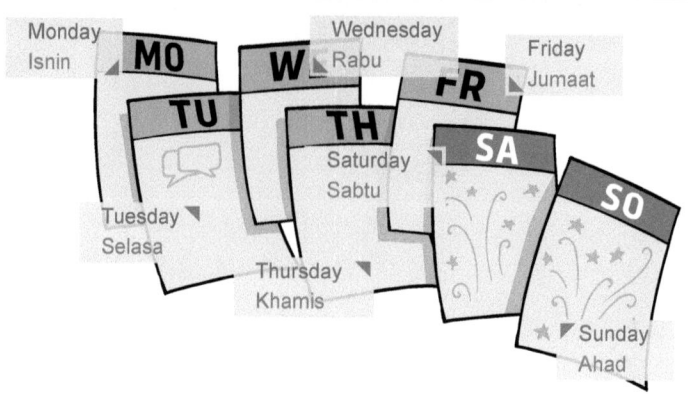

Monday
Isnin

Wednesday
Rabu

Friday
Jumaat

Tuesday
Selasa

Saturday
Sabtu

Thursday
Khamis

Sunday
Ahad

yesterday

semalam

today

hari ini

tomorrow

esok

morning

pagi

noon

tengah hari

evening

petang

MO	TU	WE	TH	FR	SA	SU
1	2	3	4	5	6	7
8	9	10	11	12	13	14
15	16	17	18	19	20	21
22	23	24	25	26	27	28
29	30	31	1	2	3	4

business days

hari kerja

MO	TU	WE	TH	FR	SA	SU
1	2	3	4	5	6	7
8	9	10	11	12	13	14
15	16	17	18	19	20	21
22	23	24	25	26	27	28
29	30	31	1	2	3	4

weekend

hari minggu

year
tahun

rain
hujan
spring
musim bunga
summer
musim panas
wind
angin
autumn
musim luruh
snow
salji
winter
musim salji

4.APRIL 11°
5.APRIL 4°
6.APRIL 13°
7.APRIL 8°
8.APRIL 10°

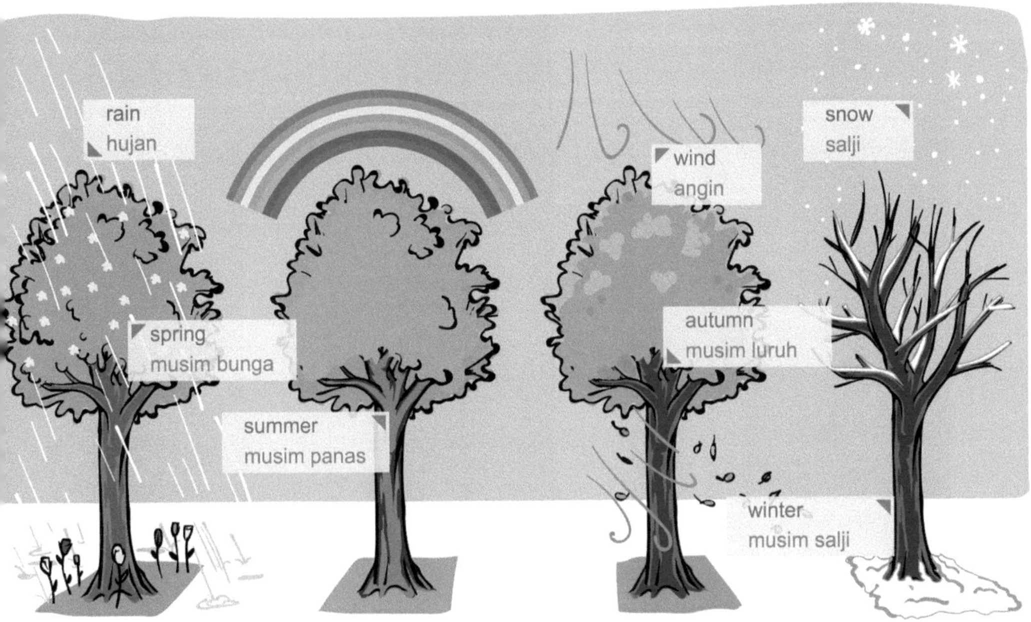

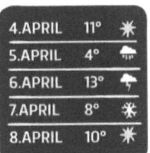

weather forecast

ramalan cuaca

F
C
120
90
60
30
0
-30
40
30
20
10
0
-10
-20

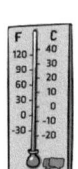

thermometer

termometer

sunshine

sinar matahari

cloud

awan

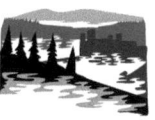

fog

kabus

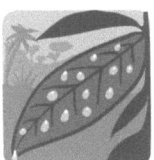

humidity

lembapan

lightning

kilat

thunder

petir

storm

ribut

hail

hujan batu

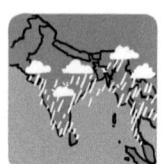

monsoon

monsun

flood

banjir

ice

ais

January

Januari

February

Februari

March

Mac

April

April

May

Mei

June

Jun

July

Julai

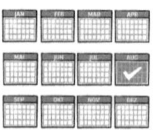

August

Ogos

year - tahun

September
....
September

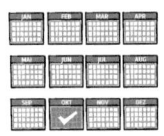

October
....
Oktober

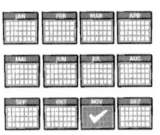

November
....
November

December
....
Disember

shapes
bentuk

circle
....
bulatan

square
....
petak

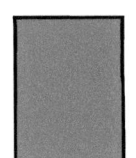

rectangle
....
segi empat tepat

triangle
....
segitiga

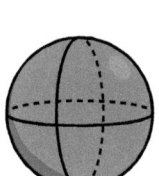

sphere
....
sfera

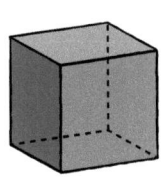

cube
....
kiub

white
....
putih

yellow
....
kuning

orange
....
oren

pink
....
merah jambu

red
....
merah

purple
....
ungu

blue
....
biru

green
....
hijau

brown
....
coklat

grey
....
kelabu

black
....
hitam

a lot / a little

banyak / sedikit

angry / calm

marah / tenang

beautiful / ugly

cantik / hodoh

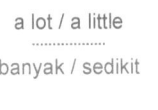

beginning / end

bermula / tamat

big / small

besar kecil

bright / dark

terang / gelap

brother / sister

abang / kakak

clean / dirty

bersih / kotor

complete / incomplete

lengkap / tidak lengkap

day / night

hari / malam

dead / alive

mati / hidup

wide / narrow

luas / sempit

edible / inedible

boleh dimakan / tidak boleh dimakan

evil / kind

jahat / baik

excited / bored

teruja / bosan

fat / thin

gemuk / kurus

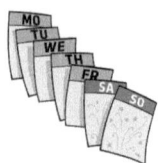

first / last

pertama / terakhir

friend / enemy

kawan / musuh

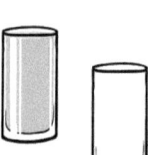

full / empty

penuh / kosong

hard / soft

keras / lembut

heavy / light

berat / ringan

hunger / thirst

lapar / dahaga

ill / healthy

sakit / sihat

illegal / legal

menyalahi undang-undang / undang-undang

intelligent / stupid

pintar / bodoh

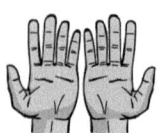

left / right

kiri / kanan

near / far

dekat / jauh

opposites - berlawanan

new / used

baru / lama

nothing / something

tiada / sesuatu

old / young

tua / muda

on / off

hidup / mati

open / closed

terbuka / tertutup

quiet / loud

diam / bising

rich / poor

kaya / miskin

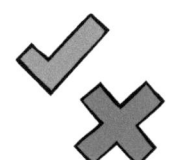

right / wrong

betul / salah

rough / smooth

kasar / halus

sad / happy

sedih / gembira

short / long

pendek / panjang

slow / fast

lambat / laju

wet / dry

basah / kering

warm / cool

panas / sejuk

war / peace

berperang / berdamai

opposites - berlawanan

0

zero

sifar

1

one

satu

2

two

dua

3

three

tiga

4

four

empat

5

five

lima

6

six

enam

7

seven

tujuh

8

eight

lapan

9

nine

sembilan

10

ten

sepuluh

11

eleven

sebelas

12

twelve

dua belas

13

thirteen

tiga belas

14

fourteen

empat belas

15

fifteen

lima belas

16

sixteen

enam belas

17

seventeen

tujuh belas

18

eighteen

lapan belas

19

nineteen

Sembilan belas

20

twenty

dua puluh

100

hundred

ratus

1.000

thousand

ribu

1.000.000

million

juta

English

Bahasa Inggeris

American English

Bahasa Inggeris Amerika

Chinese Mandarin

Bahasa Cina Mandarin

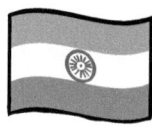

Hindi

Bahasa Hindi

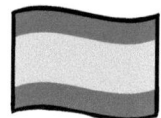

Spanish

Bahasa Sepanyol

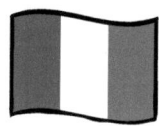

French

Bahasa Perancis

Arabic

Bahasa Arab

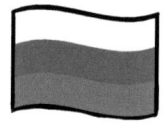

Russian

Bahasa Rusia

Portuguese

Bahasa Portugis

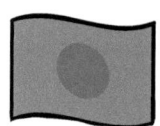

Bengali

Bahasa Benggali

German

Bahasa Jerman

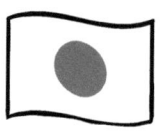

Japanese

Bahasa Jepun

I

saya

you

anda

he / she / it

dia / dia / ia

we

kita

you

anda

they

mereka

who?

siapa?

what?

apa?

how?

bagaimana?

where?

di mana?

when?

bila?

name

nama

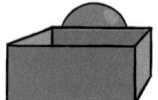

behind

belakang

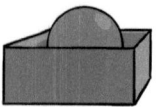

in

dalam

in front of

di hadapan

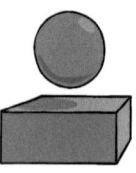

over

lebih

on

pada

under

di bawah

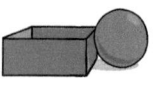

beside

bersebelahan

between

antara

place

tempat